? Essential Question
Where do good ideas come from?

Clever Puss

by Yvonne Morrin
illustrated by Kieran Rynhart

Chapter 1

Puss Wants Boots

Once there were three brothers. They lived together in a cottage with their father and his dearly loved cat. One afternoon, the father sent for his three sons.

"You're all grown now," he said. "You're old enough to go out and get jobs. I'm going on a journey, but I have gifts for you." The father gave each of his two older sons a bag filled with money.

The youngest son then stepped forward. His father said, "Tom, it's with wonderful pleasure that I give you my greatest treasure!" Then he thrust his cat into Tom's arms.

The father then patted the cat and waved farewell to his dear sons.

The next day, the two older sons disappeared to spend their riches, and poor Tom had only the cat for company.

"What a terrible treasure!" Tom cried. "You're absolutely no use to me."

The cat smiled. "I made your father's fortune," he said. "I can make you money, too. Get me a pair of boots, and you'll soon see."

Tom was now curious. "Certainly, Puss," he said. "Then you can make me wealthy like my brothers."

So Tom traded some clothes for a tiny pair of boots. The cat was delighted.

Weeks passed by, and nothing happened. Tom noticed that he was running out of food. The food that was left was stale.

"Come on, Puss," Tom kept saying. "Make me rich!"

The cat just smiled.

"This is hopeless!" Tom cried. "It's time that cat disappeared, too!"

STOP AND CHECK

What is Tom's problem in the story?

Chapter 2

The Contest

Tom opened the door to put out the cat. On the porch was a piece of paper.

"I've been expecting this!" Puss said as he read the paper. "I'm going to brainstorm some ideas." Then he disappeared inside.

Tom looked at the paper. It announced that the king was having an official contest.

The king thought that it was time he chose a successor. He had set up a contest to find his strongest, speediest citizen. The winner would become the new king.

"You must enter the contest," Puss told Tom.

"But I'm not strong or speedy!" Tom protested.

"Do as I say, and you'll be successful," Puss explained.

The next afternoon, an enormous crowd gathered at the palace to watch the contest.

Tom waited nervously. He stared at the three other contestants. They looked strong and speedy.

Soon the king announced the first contest. "You will throw a ball up into the air. You must be able to count to ten before it lands!"

The first contestant managed to count to eight before her ball landed. The second contestant counted to nine. The third contestant counted to ten before his ball hit the ground.

"I won't even make it to six," Tom muttered. The cat then whispered in his ear.

Tom nodded in agreement and then he threw his ball into the air. "Two, four, six, eight, TEN!" he cried before the ball landed.

"How inventive!" the king exclaimed. He declared that both Tom and the third contestant had successfully made it to the next round.

The losing contestants were astonished.

"Counting in twos is still counting," Tom said nervously.

STOP AND CHECK

Why is Tom nervous?

Chapter 3

A New King

"The next contest is a race," announced the king. "You must run around the castle, carrying a full bag. The first contestant to reach the finish line will be the new

While Tom and the other contestant warmed up, the cat checked out the bags and the racetrack. When he returned, he whispered in Tom's ear.

Tom and the other man stepped forward to choose their bags. The other contestant chose a light bag that was full of sponges. Tom chose a heavy bag that was full of salt.

"Go!" shouted the king.

The other contestant was ahead of Tom for most of the race. When they came to a river, the man jumped in and started swimming frantically. His sponges filled with water and became very heavy. The man started to swim more slowly because of his heavy load.

When Tom jumped in the river the salt in his bag dissolved in the water and disappeared. His bag became light, and he was able to cross the river and reach the finish line first.

The king declared Tom the winner.

"Fantastic!" Tom cried. "I am the new king. I don't have to live with that annoying cat!"

Then Tom turned to Puss and said, "I don't need your services anymore."

Although Puss said nothing, the king saw that the cat's ears were flattened in annoyance.

"Not so fast," the king said to Tom. "You may have won, but I know who had the original ideas. It was Clever Puss. He whispered in your ear. A king must be gracious like Puss, and you're a poor winner. Puss will be the new king!"

So Clever Puss moved into the palace. He really was a gracious cat. He didn't get too big for his boots. He offered Tom a job at the palace. Tom unhappily accepted it. He is now the king's royal boot polisher!

STOP AND CHECK

What idea helped Tom to win the race?

Respond to Reading

Summarize

Use important details from *Clever Puss* to summarize the story. Your graphic organizer may help you.

Character

Setting

Beginning
↓
Middle
↓
End

Text Evidence

1. How do you know that this is a fairy tale? Identify two features that tell you this. GENRE

2. What events led to Puss being left with Tom? SEQUENCE

3. What is a synonym for the word *fortune* on page 4? SYNONYMS

4. Write about the events that led up to Tom entering the contest to become the next king. WRITE ABOUT READING

Compare Texts

Read about how Rabbit tricked Fox.

Rabbit and the Well

One day, Rabbit and Fox were weeding the garden. Rabbit was thinking about how he could disappear for a nap.

Suddenly, he had an idea. "Ouch!" he cried. "I've got a thorn in my paw. I need to get it out."

As Rabbit limped off, Fox looked at him suspiciously. He thought Rabbit was up to something. After all, Fox was a trickster, too.

Soon Rabbit walked past a well. A bucket hung at the top of the well.

"That's a wonderful place for a nap," Rabbit said. "No one will discover me there!"

So he hopped into the bucket. Suddenly, it plunged into the well. A second bucket raced past it on the way up. Rabbit found himself stuck at the bottom.

"Oh well," he said. "While I'm down here, I may as well take that nap."

After a while, Rabbit heard Fox hollering his name. "I'm down here, Fox!" shouted Rabbit.

Fox peered into the well. "What are you doing?" he asked.

"Fishing!" Rabbit replied, cunningly. "Come join me."

Fox was hungry, so he jumped into the empty bucket. But Fox was heavier than Rabbit. As soon as he got into the bucket, he plunged into the well while Rabbit's bucket rose to the top.

Then Rabbit jumped out of the well. "Happy fishing!" he called to Fox as he hopped away. Finally, he knew that Fox wouldn't interrupt his afternoon nap!

Make Connections

How did Rabbit trick Fox in the story?
ESSENTIAL QUESTION

How is Rabbit in *Rabbit and the Well* similar to Puss in *Clever Puss*? How is he different? **TEXT TO TEXT**

Focus on Genre

Fairy Tales Fairy tales have imaginary settings and characters. They usually take place long ago. They sometimes include talking animals and other magical creatures. Authors sometimes write updated versions of fairy tales that add a new twist to the plot.

Read and Find *Clever Puss* is a new version of an old fairy tale. The story takes place long ago in an imaginary kingdom, and it includes a talking cat.

Your Turn

Choose a fairy tale that you know. Change the setting and characters to make them more modern. Make a two-column chart. In one column, list the features of your traditional fairy tale. In the other column, list the ways these have been used in your modern fairy tale. Some will be the same; some will be different. When you have completed the chart, share it with a classmate.

Traditional Fairy Tale	Modern Fairy Tale